SILENT DAYS,
SILENT DREAMS

ALLEN SAY

Arthur A. Levine Books

An Imprint of Scholastic Inc.

Library of Congress Cataloging-in-Publication Data
Names: Say, Allen, author.
Title: Silent days, silent dreams / Allen Say.
Description: First edition. | New York, NY : Arthur A. Levine Books, An
Imprint of Scholastic Inc., [2017] | Summary: A fictional biography of
James Castle, a deaf, autistic artist whose drawings hang in major
museums throughout the world. | Includes bibliographical references.
Identifiers: LCCN 2017017323| ISBN 9780545927611 (hardback)
Subjects: LCSH: Castle, James, 1899-1977—Juvenile fiction. | CYAC: Castle,
James, 1899-1977—Fiction. | Artists—Fiction. | Deaf—Fiction. | People
with disabilities—Fiction. | BISAC: JUVENILE NONFICTION / Biography &
Autobiography / Art. | JUVENILE NONFICTION / Art / Drawing. | JUVENILE
NONFICTION / Social Issues / Special Needs.
Classification: LCC PZ7.S2744 Sk 2017 | DDC [E]—
dc23 LC record available at https://lccn.loc.gov/2017017323

10 9 8 7 6 5 4 3 2 1   17 18 19 20 21
Printed in China 38
First edition, November 2017

Book design by Charles Kreloff and David Saylor

For Cort

JAMES CASTLE was born on September 25, 1899, on a farm in Garden Valley, Idaho. I think I knew him as well as anyone could know him — which wasn't very much — but I want to tell how I remember him. He was my uncle.

James opened his eyes to the world and saw things that moved and things that were still. Anything that moved seemed to scare him. He cried as his parents bobbed around him with darting eyes and flapping mouths. But James couldn't hear himself shrieking. For him the world would always be silent.

Like a small visitor in a museum, he stared at the unmoving faces in frames hanging on the walls.

His father was the postmaster of their small community; the Castle living room served as a post office and a general store.

James played with catalogs, books, stamped envelopes, and packages that cluttered the mail room. One day he discovered pencils and started to draw.

His parents gave him scrap paper to keep him occupied.

Soon, James was old enough to start school. On the way there, he stopped at every road sign to figure out what it meant. He never found out, but later he would put made-up signs in his drawings, which no one knew what to make of so they called them totems.

James saw more people than he had ever seen before — all with darting eyes and flapping mouths. From that day he would always be afraid of strangers.

13

James scared everyone with shrieks he couldn't hear.

His father slapped him and locked him up in the attic. "Jimmy's quiet time," the father told the family.

One afternoon, when James was let out after a long "quiet time," he looked for a place to hide. He sneaked up into the loft of the unused icehouse and saw a living picture framed by the open door.

James collected trash paper around the farm and drew on it with burnt matchsticks.
He drew everything from memory and hid the drawings in the walls of his first studio.

His father tried to make him work on the farm, but James only got in everybody's way. Finally he was left alone to play while the family worked. They called him Dummy. James couldn't hear, but he saw what it meant on their faces.

James spent so much time in the attic that it got to be his room. When his mother put a mattress on the floor, he drew the kind of bed he wanted instead. Then he drew all the things he wanted and put them in an imaginary house of his own. He lined up the drawings against the attic walls. It must have looked like a kind of gallery in there.

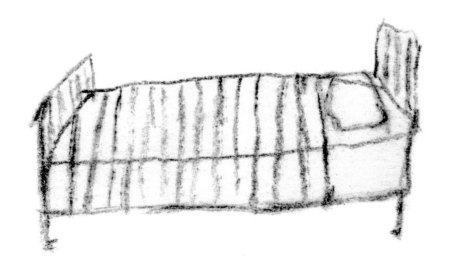

Nellie, the second eldest of James's sisters, had been born with hearing, but when she was six or seven, measles made her deaf. When James was ten, he and Nellie were sent to attend the Idaho School for the Deaf and the Blind in Gooding, about 160 miles from Garden Valley.

Seventeen-year-old Nellie turned out to be a model student; James failed at everything. But Nellie told me about the two discoveries her kid brother made at the school that changed him for good.

Gooding September 11

Dear Mama and Papa,

We are fine. Jimmy is in the boys' dormitory and I don't see him after classes. I think he likes the big buildings with so many rooms. They are like palaces. I like my room and the other girls are very nice. I will write soon.

Your loving daughter,

Nellie

One was the school library: a room with the walls covered with books like gorgeous wallpaper.

Then he saw a teacher sewing together a book — the way his mother sewed clothes at home. The woman was making textbooks for her students. Other teachers did the same. James never tired of watching them.

For James, I think books were beautiful packages of secrets that he could never puzzle out. So he drew in them — to illustrate and put his mark on pages of strange signs and symbols, and make them his books. Nellie wrote home:

When Jimmy missed classes, I got notes from his teachers. He liked the library. He couldn't read but he liked to look at the pretty books. The teachers made our textbooks there. The students read them, Jimmy drew in them.

He did the same with other students: Drawing them was his way of making friends.

Art classes were given only to the girls. That made James even more secretive.

And when the teachers caught him drawing, they were upset; they thought he was making fun of them and the students who couldn't see or hear.

They took away all his drawing things. James ran away.

Each time, he was caught and brought back and made to copy out the alphabets and numerals over and over. The odd thing was that he seemed to like the punishment. He drew them endlessly — in the same way he drew everything else. Maybe he thought he was in art class.

It wasn't surprising that he eventually invented his own alphabets and signs.

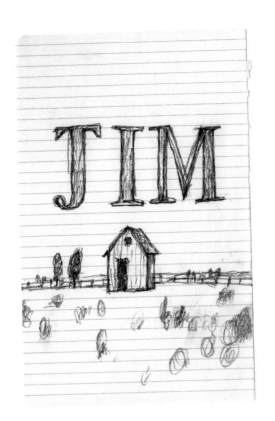

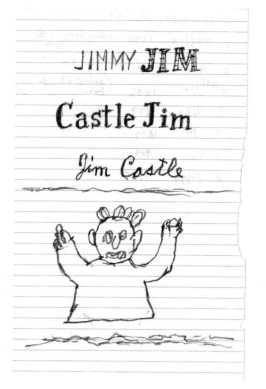

JIMMY **JIM**

Castle Jim

Jim Castle

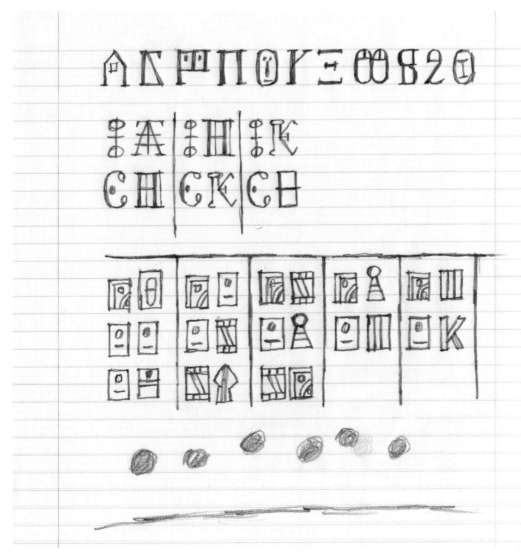

James was good with his hands and he did well in shoe-repair class. But the school couldn't teach him to speak. Finally the principal wrote to Mr. Castle that James was "ineducable." He was fifteen.

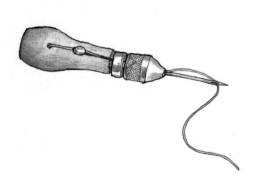

The principal warned Mr. Castle not to give James any drawing materials at home.
He said James should learn to read and write and not waste time on drawings.

One morning, as James's older brother, Joe, cleaned the chimney, he noticed James watching him. Later, their mother told Joe that Jimmy had taken some soot in a jar, and to see what he was up to.

"He's smearing soot with his spit," Joe reported. "He's drawing on junk paper and making books out of them. Craziest looking books you ever saw, all trash. You'd think he's finally learned to read!"

James drew everything he saw around the farm and decorated his studio with artwork. He drew a lot of imaginary houses with his name on them.

By then, James had two younger sisters, and there were seven kids altogether. One time his brother Joe stole some drawings and showed them to the girls.

"He finally learned his name!" They laughed. "Jimmy's Dream House!"

"Look, he's made friends for himself!"

James stayed in his studio to guard it from invaders. And whenever he caught
Joe and his friends trying to raid his room, he let out piercing screams and chased
them away. And "Dummy" got his second mean nickname: Crazy Jimmy.

In 1923, James's parents sold the farm in Garden Valley and bought a smaller farm in Star, Idaho. All of James's artwork was left behind in the icehouse loft.

At the new place, James turned an empty shed into his second studio.

Mr. Castle died four years later. Only Mrs. Castle, James, and his youngest sister, Peggy, were left at the farm. When Peggy married and had a baby girl, Mrs. Castle sold the farm and together they moved to Boise.

Again, all of James's artwork, which he had carefully wrapped in packages, was left behind.

In the new house, Peggy had three more children. Her husband, Guy, put a cot
and a desk and a little woodstove in the old, abandoned chicken house for James.

Lonely for friends, he made cutout dolls, farm animals, and birds out of cardboard saved from trash bins.

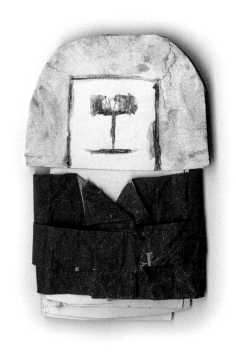

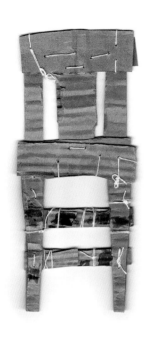  

He made furniture out of cardboard — even a window — and turned the
chicken house into his third studio, which was also his first real bedroom.

It wasn't long before the neighborhood kids discovered Crazy Jimmy's studio and trashed it while he was out. After each raid came a terrible scream.

Finally, James took an armload of his work . . .

. . . and made several trips to the nearby canal.

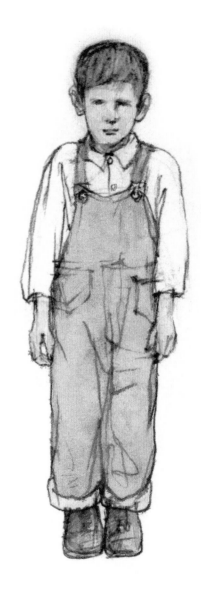

But James liked kids, and he was friendly to anyone who showed interest in his work — even though that didn't happen often. I'm the only one he ever allowed in his studio because he knew I liked to watch him draw. Besides, my mom, Emma, is his next-younger sister, two years older than Peggy. Even though he couldn't hear me, I called him Uncle Jim.

He never knew my name is Bob.

My family moved to Washington when I was thirteen, and after high school I joined the Army. I thought a lot about Uncle Jim. There was no use in writing to him: My letters would be just scrap paper for him to draw on.

As soon as I was a civilian again, I went to Oregon and enrolled in an art school in Portland, where, to tell the truth, I was just an OK student.

The professor didn't notice me until I showed him some drawings that Uncle Jim had given me. He got very excited.

"Where is this artist hiding? I've got to meet him!"

Uncle Jim was going to get me an A from the hardest professor at the school!

I agreed to drive him to Boise. I hadn't seen my uncle in ten years and hoped he wasn't still living in the chicken house.

The professor babbled more than usual. He took away examples of
Uncle's art and organized an exhibit of it back at the school in Portland.

So Uncle Jim had his first one-man show at my school and he never knew about it.

Then a gallery in Portland sold some pictures. Newspapers wrote reviews about the amazing art made by a deaf artist who was completely self-taught. The sales of Uncle's work excited Auntie Peggy very much.

Then Bob Clay, the director of the Boise Gallery of Art, heard the news.

"They're talking about a local artist!" he exclaimed.

Mr. Clay visited Uncle Jim at Peggy's house. He brought with him a drawing pad and soon the two men were drawing each other in it. Then Uncle Jim showed him his studio. The chicken coop depressed the director, but the artwork so impressed him that he promised to put up a show at the gallery.

He asked Peggy not to bring James to the
gallery in his overalls, but was still surprised
when he showed up in a silk suit. Mr. Clay said
James was the sharpest one at the opening.

The turnout was good and a few pieces were sold. Reporters and photographers hovered around the artist. He stayed long after everyone was gone, looking at his work all in frames, rocking slowly in his new shoes.

Peggy was happy when some galleries started selling his work. Then she worried about people seeing where her brother lived and worked. She took him to a used trailer dealer.

Uncle Jim drew a picture of Peggy with wheels for feet, which she didn't understand. After a lot of growling from Uncle, she bought him a two-room mobile home and a television, and I heard him laugh for the first time. He could laugh like anyone else!

After thirty years in the chicken coop, Uncle Jim finally got his
Dream House, as the family called it. He worked in it for fifteen
more years, in the same way he had when I was a kid — drawing
with soot and spit on scavenged paper. I think he was happy.

58

Author's Note

Four years ago, Cort Conley, a friend who lives in Idaho, asked if I would draw a portrait of a local artist there; he wanted to donate it to a library. We've been friends for over fifty years; I had borrowed money from him. I agreed to do a drawing, and he sent a photo of the artist and a catalog of his work.

It was my introduction to James Castle, an artist I didn't know.

I opened the catalog and suddenly remembered the excitement of seeing a van Gogh for the first time. I was twelve and the van Gogh was a poster, but I was seeing a painting for the first time and it was a living thing.

Now the catalog made me sit up. Who was James Castle? How did he come to make such startlingly original art? I skimmed through the text and traced out a thumbnail biography.

He was born two months premature on September 25, 1899, on a farm in Garden Valley, Idaho. He was deaf, mute, autistic, and probably dyslexic, yet he managed to teach himself to draw. He spent five years at the Idaho School for the Deaf and the Blind, but never learned to speak, read, write, or use sign language. Deprived of drawing materials, he drew on wastepaper with sharpened sticks dipped in spit and soot. For thirty years he worked in an abandoned chicken house, then fifteen more years in a two-room mobile home. He died on October 26, 1977, and left more than 15,000 pieces of artwork.

Not an eventful life. I asked Cort for more information and soon my workroom became cluttered with piles of publications. I read a biography and essays, watched taped interviews of his surviving relatives and art critics and dealers. They told conflicting stories.

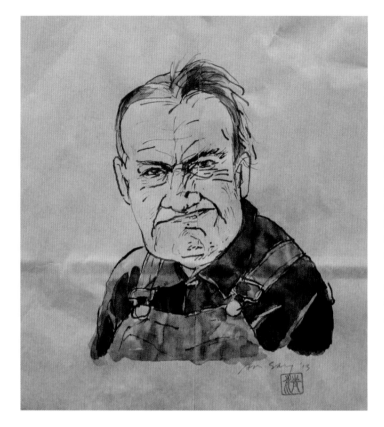

We know a great deal about van Gogh from the letters he wrote to his brother, Theo. He painted everything from life, even the stars at night. James Castle had no words; he drew from memory and in secrecy. He was called abusive names like Crazy Jimmy, the Dummy, and the Retard.

I was also called a dummy when I first came to America. Not knowing English in California felt the same as being deaf and mute. Now I wanted to dig out my buried memory and try to see the young James's silent world through his eyes. And so began this book.

But first I had to keep my promise to Cort — an ardent fan of "Jimmy" as Theo was of Vincent. I didn't use the photo he sent but sketched from a head-on shot in the catalog. It's a caricature drawn on a used shopping bag, as James might have done. But as I began work on the book, I had second thoughts: I would do a proper portrait when I knew him better.

I studied his drawings. None of them has a sun or a moon or a single flower — things one always sees in children's art, and in van Gogh's. His pictures look like sketched frames of a silent movie. He made cardboard dolls, which his family called his friends. Almost all his landscapes have houses in them — "Jimmy's Dream House" was a family joke. He drew the alphabet and numerals backward and forward as if to work out the puzzles that only he couldn't solve. And perhaps out of jealousy, he created his own calligraphy, which no one could read, and made hundreds of books and albums with which he filled his studio.

It was like interviewing five or six very busy artists who worked in different media. His range was too large for a picture book, so I decided to concentrate mostly on his drawings.

As a boy, when his pencils were taken away, James drew with burnt matchsticks. I found them richer in colors than drawing charcoals, but powdery and unstable. Fixative was unknown to James, so whatever he had drawn with them rubbed off. I tried a sharpened stick — his favorite tool — dipping it in soot mixed with spit, and discovered that saliva is a natural fixative! This explains how thousands of his drawings survived.

To emulate his unschooled style, I used the same kinds of odd materials he had used: soot and spit, liquid laundry bluing, and shoe polish, to name a few.

I had help. My wife meticulously made dolls and birds out of wastepaper and cardboard that I think the artist would have approved. I drew on ninety-year-old letters and envelopes that Cort found in an antique shop; and to mimic James's unsteady lines, I often switched hands — to my left hand, which hadn't learned to tell lies.

Burnt matchsticks are interesting to draw with, but they are too delicate. I hate to think of all the early James Castle drawings that got wiped off. For two days, my studio stank from the burnt sulfur.

These are some of the tools I used to make this book. In addition, I used cotton wads, rags, Q-tips, big nails, toothpicks, brushes, and my fingers.

Drawing, like making mud pies or dancing for joy, is a natural play activity for children: No lessons are needed to get them going. James got going on his own and kept going for seventy years in isolation — only two persons were known to have watched him draw; one was his nephew, Robert Beach.

After he died, as with van Gogh, much of what he had made turned out to be works of art. My teacher, Noro Shinpei, had said that the artist's time in the studio is time in paradise. For James, I think life was one long silent dream, which he recorded for himself, and unintentionally for the world.

He moved three times and never left Idaho. The cache of more than 15,000 pieces of artwork he left is thought to be about one-third of his total output. At that, it is an immense diary of a person who thought entirely in pictures. And today the diary is scattered in loose pages and sold piecemeal in the art market.

I learned all this through my friend Cort. The portrait I promised him has turned into a book. It's an imagined biography of a most original and enigmatic artist, whose fame continues to grow.

Allen Say

Bibliography

Bell, Nicholas R., and Leslie Umberger. *Untitled: The Art of James Castle*. With a foreword by Alexander Nemerov. London: GILES, 2014. Published in conjunction with the exhibition of the same name, shown at the Smithsonian American Art Museum.

Cooke, Lynne, ed. *James Castle: Show and Store*. New York: Distributed Art Publishers, in association with Museo Nacional Centro de Arte Reina Sofia, 2011. Published in conjunction with the exhibition of the same name, shown at the Museo Nacional Centro de Arte Reina Sofia.

Del Deo, Frank. "Sum of its parts: The constructions of James Castle." In *James Castle: Structures*. New York: Knoedler & Company, in association with J Crist Gallery, 2002. Published in conjunction with the exhibition of the same name shown at J Crist Gallery.

Galerie Karsten Greve. *James Castle*. Cologne: Galerie Karsten Greve, 2011. Published in conjunction with the exhibition of the same name shown at Galerie Karsten Greve.

Grigley, Joseph. "Right at home: James Castle and the slow life drawing." In *James Castle*. Dublin: Douglas Hyde Gallery, 2010. Published in conjunction with the exhibition of the same name shown at Douglas Hyde Gallery.

Harthorn, Sandy. "A voice of silence." In *A Voice of Silence: A Retrospective of Works by James Castle*. Boise: Boise Gallery of Art, 1982. Published in conjunction with the exhibition of the same name shown at Boise Gallery of Art.

Jon, Dennis Michael. *James Castle: The Experience of Every Day*, Minneapolis; Minneapolis Institute of Arts, 2016. Published in conjunction with the exhibition of the same name shown at Minneapolis Institute of Arts.

Knoedler & Company. *James Castle / Walker Evans: Word-Play, Signs and Symbols*. With an essay by Stephen Westfall. New York: Knoedler & Company, in association with J Crist Gallery, 2006. Published in conjunction with the exhibition of the same name shown at J Crist Gallery.

Knoedler & Company. *James Castle Drawings: Vision and Touch*. With an essay by Margit Rowell. New York: Knoedler & Company, in association with J Crist Gallery, 2009. Published in conjunction with the exhibition of the same name shown at J Crist Gallery.

Nickas, Bob. "James Castle: Book with the sound of its own meaning." In *James Castle: Books*. San Antonio: Lawrence Markey, Inc. 2010. Published in conjunction with the exhibition of the same name, shown at Lawrence Markey Gallery.

Percy, Ann. ed. *James Castle: A Retrospective*. New Haven: Yale University Press, in association with Philadelphia Museum of Art, 2008. Published in conjunction with the exhibition of the same name, shown at the Philadelphia Museum of Art.

Rowell, Margit. "Vision and Touch: James Castle Drawings." In *James Castle Drawings: Vision and Touch*. New York: Knoedler & Company, in association with J Crist Gallery, 2009. Published in conjunction with the exhibition of the same name shown at J Crist Gallery.

Tayloe Piggott Gallery. *James Castle: An Absence of There*. With essay by Frank Del Deo. Jackson: Tayloe Piggott Gallery, 2012. Published in conjunction with the exhibition of the same name shown at Tayloe Piggott Gallery.

Tobler, Jay. "James Castle: House Drawings." In *Drawing Papers 6*. New York: The Drawing Center, 2000. Published in conjunction with the exhibition of the same name shown at The Drawing Center.

Trusky, Tom. *James Castle: His Life & Art*. Boise: Idaho Center for the Book, 2008.